# The Power of Com
# Teams and Boostin

## Gyula

# Copyright © [2023]

## Title: The Power of Connection Building Stronger Teams and Boosting Employee Engagement

## Author's: Gyula.

This book was printed and published by [Publisher's: Gyula]  in [2023]

ISBN:

# TABLE OF CONTENTS

# Chapter 3: Communicating Effectively for Engagement

The Power of Transparent Communication

Listening and Empathy: Keys to Effective Communication

Providing Feedback and Recognition

Encouraging Two-Way Communication

Leveraging Technology for Communication

# Chapter 4: Creating a Sense of Belonging and Connection

Promoting Collaboration and Teamwork

Building Relationships and Trust

Celebrating Diversity and Inclusion

Developing a Sense of Community

Encouraging Social Connections

# Chapter 5: Empowering Employees for Engagement

Giving Autonomy and Ownership

Providing Meaningful Work

Supporting Work-Life Balance

Encouraging Innovation and Creativity

Recognizing and Rewarding Contributions

# Chapter 9: The Future of Employee Engagement

Trends and Innovations in Employee Engagement

Adapting to a Changing Workforce

Embracing Technology for Engagement

The Role of Artificial Intelligence in Engagement

Cultivating a Culture of Lifelong Engagement

# Chapter 10: Conclusion: Taking Action for Lasting Engagement

Reflecting on the Power of Connection

Creating a Personalized Engagement Plan

Committing to Continuous Improvement

Inspiring Others to Build Stronger Teams

Empowering Employees for a Brighter Future

# Chapter 1: The Importance of Employee Engagement

## Understanding Employee Engagement

Employee engagement is a critical factor for the success and growth of any organization. It refers to the emotional commitment and involvement of employees towards their work, the organization, and its goals. When employees are engaged, they are not just physically present at work; they are enthusiastic, motivated, and dedicated to delivering their best.

In today's competitive business environment, understanding and fostering employee engagement is essential for organizations to thrive. This subchapter aims to provide a comprehensive understanding of employee engagement, its importance, and how it can be nurtured to build stronger teams and boost overall organizational performance.

To begin with, employee engagement is not a one-size-fits-all concept. It varies from person to person and organization to organization. However, there are common factors that contribute to employee engagement, such as clear communication, effective leadership, recognition and rewards, opportunities for growth and development, and a positive work environment. By acknowledging and addressing these factors, organizations can create an environment that fosters high levels of engagement.

Engaged employees are more likely to be proactive, innovative, and willing to go the extra mile to achieve organizational goals. They exhibit higher levels of job satisfaction, which leads to reduced turnover rates and increased productivity. Moreover, engaged employees are brand ambassadors, promoting the organization's values and culture both within and outside the workplace.

This subchapter will delve into the various dimensions of employee engagement, including the role of leadership in driving engagement, the impact of organizational culture, the significance of employee well-being, and the correlation between engagement and performance. It will also explore strategies and best practices for enhancing employee engagement at all levels of an organization.

By understanding the underlying principles and dynamics of employee engagement, individuals and organizations can cultivate an environment that fosters strong connections, collaboration, and commitment. Whether you are a manager seeking to boost employee morale or an employee looking to enhance your own engagement, this subchapter will serve as a valuable resource.

In conclusion, employee engagement is vital for organizational success and requires a deep understanding of its drivers and implications. This subchapter aims to equip readers with the knowledge and tools to enhance employee engagement, build stronger teams, and create a culture of high performance. By investing in employee engagement, organizations can unlock the untapped potential of their workforce and thrive in today's competitive landscape.

# The Link between Employee Engagement and Organizational Success

Employee engagement is a critical factor in the success of any organization. It refers to the emotional commitment and dedication that employees have towards their work and the organization. When employees are engaged, they are more likely to go above and beyond their regular job duties, contribute innovative ideas, and actively seek ways to improve their performance and the organization as a whole.

In today's competitive business landscape, organizations that prioritize employee engagement have a significant advantage. Engaged employees are more productive, creative, and motivated. They are also more likely to stay with the organization, reducing turnover rates and associated costs. Moreover, engaged employees are strong advocates for the organization, promoting its products or services and attracting top talent.

So, how can organizations foster employee engagement? It starts with effective leadership and management practices. When leaders create a positive work environment, provide clear expectations, and support their employees' professional growth, they lay the foundation for engagement. Moreover, leaders who communicate openly and honestly, recognize and appreciate their employees' contributions, and involve them in decision-making processes, create a sense of trust and commitment that fuels engagement.

Another crucial aspect of employee engagement is the alignment between individual and organizational goals. When employees understand how their work contributes to the organization's success and feel that their efforts are valued, they are more likely to be engaged. Organizations can achieve this by implementing transparent performance management systems, providing regular feedback, and offering opportunities for growth and development.

Furthermore, fostering a culture of collaboration and teamwork is essential for employee engagement. When employees feel connected to their colleagues and work in a supportive and inclusive environment, they are more likely to be engaged. Organizations can promote collaboration by creating cross-functional teams, organizing team-building activities, and encouraging open communication and knowledge sharing.

In conclusion, employee engagement is a critical driver of organizational success. Engaged employees are more productive, innovative, and loyal, contributing to the overall growth and profitability of the organization. To foster employee engagement, organizations must focus on effective leadership, aligning individual and organizational goals, and promoting a culture of collaboration. By investing in employee engagement, organizations can build stronger teams and create a thriving work environment that drives organizational success.

This subchapter of "The Power of Connection: Building Stronger Teams and Boosting Employee Engagement" explores the link between employee engagement and organizational success. It provides insights and practical strategies for individuals and organizations interested in improving employee engagement and maximizing their organizational performance. Whether you are a business leader, human resources professional, or an employee looking to enhance your engagement at work, this subchapter offers valuable guidance to help you unleash the power of employee engagement in your organization.

# The Consequences of Low Employee Engagement

In today's fast-paced and competitive business world, employee engagement has become a critical factor in determining the success or failure of an organization. Low employee engagement can have far-reaching consequences that can negatively impact both the individual and the organization as a whole. This subchapter explores the various repercussions of low employee engagement and sheds light on the importance of addressing this issue in the realm of organizational behavior.

One of the most significant consequences of low employee engagement is decreased productivity. When employees are not engaged in their work, they are more likely to be disinterested, unmotivated, and less committed to achieving organizational goals. As a result, their performance suffers, leading to reduced productivity levels. This can have a detrimental effect on the overall success of the organization, hindering growth and profitability.

Another consequence of low employee engagement is increased turnover rates. When employees do not feel connected to their work or valued by the organization, they are more likely to seek opportunities elsewhere. High turnover rates can be incredibly costly for organizations, both in terms of recruitment and training expenses, as well as the loss of valuable institutional knowledge. Moreover, a revolving door of employees can negatively impact team dynamics and morale, leading to a further decline in engagement levels.

Low employee engagement also has a direct impact on employee well-being. When individuals are disengaged, they are more likely to experience stress, burnout, and a decreased sense of job satisfaction. This can lead to a decline in mental and physical health, resulting in increased absenteeism and presenteeism. Ultimately, the well-being of employees is crucial not only for their personal fulfillment but also for the overall success of the organization.

Furthermore, low employee engagement can tarnish an organization's reputation. In today's interconnected world, where information spreads rapidly through social media and online platforms, disgruntled employees can easily share their negative experiences. This can damage an organization's employer brand, making it challenging to attract and retain top talent.

To address the consequences of low employee engagement, organizations must prioritize strategies and initiatives aimed at boosting engagement levels. By fostering a culture of connection, communication, and collaboration, organizations can create an environment where employees feel valued, motivated, and empowered. This, in turn, leads to increased productivity, higher employee retention rates, enhanced employee well-being, and a positive employer brand reputation.

In conclusion, low employee engagement can have severe consequences for both individuals and organizations. By recognizing the importance of employee engagement and taking proactive steps to address it, organizations can build stronger teams, boost employee engagement, and ultimately achieve success in today's competitive business landscape.

# The Benefits of High Employee Engagement

Employee engagement has become a buzzword in the world of organizational behavior, and for good reason. When employees are engaged, they are more committed, motivated, and productive. In this subchapter, we will explore the numerous benefits that high employee engagement can bring to organizations of all sizes and industries.

One of the key benefits of high employee engagement is increased productivity. Engaged employees are more likely to go above and beyond in their work, and they have a higher level of job satisfaction. When employees are engaged, they are more focused and motivated, leading to improved efficiency and effectiveness in their tasks. This increased productivity can have a direct impact on the bottom line, as organizations with engaged employees tend to outperform their competitors.

Furthermore, high employee engagement leads to improved customer satisfaction. Engaged employees are more likely to deliver exceptional customer service, as they genuinely care about their work and the impact they have on customers. When employees are engaged, they are more attentive, responsive, and empathetic, resulting in positive customer experiences and increased customer loyalty.

Another benefit of high employee engagement is reduced turnover. Engaged employees are more committed to their organizations and are less likely to seek opportunities elsewhere. They feel a sense of purpose and belonging, which leads to higher levels of job satisfaction and loyalty. This reduced turnover not only saves organizations the costs associated with hiring and training new employees but also helps maintain continuity and stability within the workforce.

Moreover, high employee engagement fosters a positive work culture. Engaged employees are more likely to collaborate, share knowledge, and support their colleagues. This creates a supportive and inclusive work environment where employees feel valued and appreciated. A positive work culture not only improves employee morale and well-being but also attracts top talent, as organizations with high employee engagement become known as desirable places to work.

In conclusion, high employee engagement brings a multitude of benefits to organizations. From increased productivity and improved customer satisfaction to reduced turnover and a positive work culture, the advantages are undeniable. By investing in employee engagement initiatives, organizations can build stronger teams, boost morale, and ultimately achieve greater success in today's competitive business landscape.

# The Role of Leadership in Employee Engagement

In today's rapidly changing business landscape, employee engagement has emerged as a critical factor for organizational success. Engaged employees are not only more productive but also more loyal, innovative, and committed to the company's goals. As leaders, it is our responsibility to foster an environment that promotes employee engagement, and in doing so, drive overall performance and growth.

Leadership plays a pivotal role in shaping employee engagement within an organization. Effective leaders create a sense of purpose and vision that inspires and motivates employees to give their best. By setting clear expectations and providing regular feedback, leaders ensure that employees understand their roles and feel valued for their contributions.

One of the key aspects of leadership that influences employee engagement is communication. Open and transparent communication builds trust and fosters a sense of belonging among employees. When leaders actively listen to their team members, address their concerns, and provide timely information, it creates a culture of transparency and encourages engagement.

Moreover, leaders must lead by example. They need to embody the values and behaviors they expect from their employees. By demonstrating integrity, accountability, and empathy, leaders create a positive work environment where employees feel supported and encouraged to reach their full potential.

Another critical role of leadership in employee engagement is providing opportunities for growth and development. Leaders should invest in training and development programs that enhance employee skills and knowledge. By offering career advancement opportunities and recognizing individual achievements, leaders show that they are committed to their employees' professional growth, which in turn boosts engagement and loyalty.

Furthermore, leaders should empower their employees by delegating responsibilities and giving them autonomy. When employees have a sense of ownership and control over their work, they feel more engaged and motivated to achieve success. By fostering a culture of empowerment, leaders encourage innovation, creativity, and initiative among their teams.

In conclusion, leadership plays a central role in driving employee engagement. Effective leaders inspire, communicate, lead by example, and provide growth opportunities, ultimately creating a work environment that fosters engagement. By prioritizing employee engagement, leaders can build stronger teams, boost productivity, and achieve organizational success.

# Chapter 2: Building a Foundation for Employee Engagement

## Defining Organizational Purpose and Values

In today's fast-paced and ever-changing business landscape, it is more important than ever for organizations to have a clear and defined purpose. An organization's purpose serves as its guiding light, providing direction and meaning to every employee's work. It is the driving force behind the organization's goals and objectives, and it shapes the decisions and actions taken at all levels. But defining and effectively communicating an organization's purpose is not an easy task. It requires a deep understanding of the organization's values and a commitment to aligning every aspect of the business with those values.

Organizational purpose goes beyond making profits or achieving financial success. It encompasses the broader impact an organization wants to have on its employees, customers, and the world. It is about creating a sense of shared meaning and inspiring employees to work towards a common goal. When every member of an organization understands and believes in its purpose, it creates a sense of unity and motivation, leading to increased employee engagement and satisfaction.

Values, on the other hand, serve as the foundation for an organization's culture and behavior. They define what the organization stands for and guide decision-making processes. Values reflect the organization's beliefs, ethics, and principles, and they shape the way employees interact with each other and with external stakeholders. When an organization's values are clearly defined and consistently upheld, it fosters a positive work environment and builds trust among all members.

Defining organizational purpose and values requires a collaborative effort that involves all stakeholders, from top-level executives to front-line employees. It is important to engage in open and transparent discussions to identify the core values that represent the organization's identity and to establish a purpose that resonates with all members. Once defined, these values and purpose must be regularly communicated and integrated into every aspect of the organization, from recruitment and training to performance evaluations and decision-making processes.

In conclusion, defining organizational purpose and values is a crucial step towards building stronger teams and boosting employee engagement. It provides a clear direction for the organization, aligns everyone towards a common goal, and fosters a positive work environment. By defining and living by these principles, organizations can create a sense of purpose and meaning that attracts and retains top talent, enhances productivity, and ultimately leads to long-term success.

# Creating a Positive Work Culture

In today's fast-paced and competitive business landscape, organizations are increasingly recognizing the importance of creating a positive work culture. A positive work culture not only promotes a healthy and happy workplace environment but also boosts employee engagement and enhances overall team performance. In this subchapter, we will explore the key elements of creating a positive work culture and how it can benefit organizations and individuals alike.

First and foremost, a positive work culture starts with strong leadership. Leaders play a crucial role in setting the tone and values of an organization. By emphasizing respect, open communication, and collaboration, leaders can create an environment where employees feel valued and supported. When leaders prioritize the well-being of their teams, it fosters a sense of trust and loyalty, leading to increased employee engagement.

Open and transparent communication is another essential element of a positive work culture. When employees feel heard and understood, they are more likely to be engaged and motivated. Regular team meetings, one-on-one check-ins, and feedback sessions are effective ways to promote open dialogue and ensure that everyone's voice is heard. Additionally, creating channels for employees to provide suggestions and share ideas not only encourages innovation but also strengthens the sense of belonging and ownership within the organization.

Recognition and appreciation are powerful tools in building a positive work culture. Acknowledging and celebrating employees' achievements and contributions boosts morale and motivation.

Whether it's through verbal praise, written recognition, or rewards and incentives, a culture of appreciation reinforces positive behaviors and creates a supportive and uplifting work environment.

Work-life balance is another vital aspect of a positive work culture. Organizations that prioritize the well-being of their employees understand the importance of allowing time for personal and family commitments. Offering flexible work arrangements, promoting self-care initiatives, and encouraging work-life integration can significantly contribute to employee satisfaction and productivity.

Lastly, fostering a sense of community and teamwork is essential in creating a positive work culture. Encouraging collaboration, team-building activities, and cross-departmental projects not only strengthens relationships but also enhances problem-solving capabilities and overall organizational performance.

In conclusion, creating a positive work culture is crucial for organizations to thrive in today's competitive landscape. By prioritizing strong leadership, open communication, recognition, work-life balance, and teamwork, organizations can boost employee engagement, enhance productivity, and create a harmonious and fulfilling workplace environment. Whether you are an employee, a team leader, or a business owner, investing in creating a positive work culture is a powerful way to build stronger teams and drive organizational success.

## Establishing Clear Expectations and Goals

In any organization, clear expectations and goals are essential for success. They provide employees with a sense of direction and purpose, allowing them to focus their efforts on achieving the desired outcomes. In this subchapter, we will explore the importance of establishing clear expectations and goals in building stronger teams and boosting employee engagement.

When expectations and goals are unclear, employees may feel lost or uncertain about what is expected of them. This can lead to confusion, frustration, and a decrease in productivity. On the other hand, when expectations and goals are clearly communicated, employees have a clear understanding of what is expected from them, which enables them to align their efforts accordingly.

Clear expectations and goals also help to create a sense of accountability within teams. When everyone is aware of the desired outcomes and their individual roles in achieving them, it becomes easier to hold each other accountable for their actions and results. This fosters a culture of responsibility and ownership, where individuals take pride in their work and strive to meet or exceed expectations.

Moreover, clear expectations and goals provide a framework for performance evaluation and feedback. When employees know what is expected of them, it becomes easier for managers to assess their performance objectively and provide feedback that is helpful and constructive. Regular feedback and performance evaluations can lead to continuous improvement and growth within the organization.

To establish clear expectations and goals, it is important to involve employees in the process. This promotes a sense of ownership and commitment to the goals. Communicating expectations and goals through multiple channels, such as team meetings, emails, and performance reviews, ensures that the message is effectively conveyed and understood.

In conclusion, establishing clear expectations and goals is crucial for building stronger teams and boosting employee engagement. By providing a sense of direction, fostering accountability, enabling performance evaluation, and involving employees in the process, organizations can create a culture of clarity, focus, and achievement. When everyone is on the same page and working towards common goals, the potential for success is limitless.

## Providing Opportunities for Growth and Development

In today's fast-paced and ever-evolving world, organizations need to prioritize the growth and development of their employees. This subchapter explores the significance of providing opportunities for growth and development in the context of organizational behavior. Whether you are a manager, team leader, or employee, understanding and implementing strategies to foster growth and development can lead to stronger teams and increased employee engagement.

One of the key benefits of providing opportunities for growth and development is the enhancement of employee skills and knowledge. By investing in training programs, workshops, and seminars, organizations can equip their employees with the necessary tools to excel in their roles. This not only benefits the individual employee but also contributes to the overall success of the organization. When employees feel supported in their professional development, they are more likely to be engaged, motivated, and productive.

Moreover, providing opportunities for growth and development can contribute to the retention of top talent. Employees who feel stagnant in their roles are more likely to seek new opportunities elsewhere. However, when organizations prioritize their employees' growth, they create a sense of loyalty and commitment. This, in turn, reduces turnover rates and saves the organization both time and resources in recruiting and training new employees.

Another important aspect to consider is the impact of growth and development on employee satisfaction and morale. When individuals are given opportunities to learn and grow, they feel valued and appreciated. This sense of fulfillment translates into higher job satisfaction and improved morale within the organization. Employees who are satisfied and engaged in their work are more likely to go above and beyond their responsibilities, resulting in better performance and outcomes for the organization as a whole.

To effectively provide opportunities for growth and development, organizations should adopt a holistic approach. This includes creating a learning culture that encourages continuous learning and exploration. Managers and team leaders should actively identify and support the development needs of their employees. This can be done through regular performance evaluations, goal-setting sessions, and personalized development plans.

In conclusion, providing opportunities for growth and development is crucial in today's organizational landscape. It not only improves individual employee skills and knowledge but also contributes to increased engagement, retention of top talent, and overall organizational success. By prioritizing growth and development, organizations can build stronger teams and foster a culture of continuous learning and improvement.

## Fostering a Supportive and Inclusive Environment

In today's fast-paced and ever-changing organizational landscape, it is crucial for companies to prioritize the creation of a supportive and inclusive environment. This subchapter delves into the importance of fostering such an environment and provides practical strategies to achieve this goal. Whether you are a team leader, a business owner, or an employee, understanding the power of connection and the impact it can have on organizational behavior is essential for building stronger teams and boosting employee engagement.

Creating a supportive and inclusive environment goes beyond simply adhering to diversity policies. It requires a genuine commitment to embracing differences and encouraging collaboration. By fostering an environment where individuals feel valued, respected, and included, organizations can tap into the full potential of their workforce, leading to increased productivity, innovation, and employee satisfaction.

One of the key strategies to foster a supportive environment is open communication. Allowing employees to express their ideas, concerns, and feedback freely promotes a sense of belonging and ownership. Organizations should encourage open dialogues and provide platforms for employees to voice their opinions, ensuring that everyone's voice is heard and valued.

Another crucial aspect is promoting diversity and inclusion. Organizations should actively seek diverse talent and create a culture where everyone feels included, regardless of their background, gender, or ethnicity. This can be achieved through training programs, mentorship initiatives, and inclusive policies that promote equal opportunities for all.

Supportive leadership is also vital in creating an inclusive environment. Leaders should lead by example, showing empathy, understanding, and respect for their team members. By fostering a culture of trust and support, leaders can empower their employees to take risks, share ideas, and collaborate effectively.

Lastly, organizations should encourage teamwork and collaboration. By fostering a collaborative environment, individuals are more likely to feel supported and motivated. Encouraging cross-functional collaboration, team-building activities, and recognizing and rewarding teamwork can boost employee morale, improve communication, and drive organizational success.

In conclusion, fostering a supportive and inclusive environment is crucial in today's organizational landscape. By prioritizing open communication, promoting diversity and inclusion, cultivating supportive leadership, and encouraging teamwork, organizations can create a culture that not only boosts employee engagement but also drives innovation, productivity, and overall success. Embracing the power of connection and understanding its impact on organizational behavior is the key to building stronger teams and nurturing a thriving work environment for everyone.

# Chapter 3: Communicating Effectively for Engagement

## The Power of Transparent Communication

### Subchapter: The Power of Transparent Communication

In today's fast-paced and interconnected world, effective communication is more crucial than ever before. Transparent communication, in particular, has emerged as a powerful tool for building stronger teams and boosting employee engagement. In this subchapter, we will explore the significance of transparent communication in the context of organizational behavior and how it can transform workplaces for the better.

Transparent communication involves sharing information openly, honestly, and without any hidden agenda. It promotes trust, collaboration, and a sense of belonging among team members. When leaders and employees communicate transparently, it creates an environment where everyone feels valued, heard, and empowered to contribute their best.

One of the key benefits of transparent communication is the establishment of trust. When leaders communicate openly and honestly, it sends a message that they trust their employees with important information. This trust fosters a sense of loyalty and commitment among employees, as they feel that their ideas and opinions are valued. Trust also enables effective decision-making processes, as individuals are more likely to share their perspectives and challenge existing norms.

Transparent communication also enhances collaboration within teams. When information is shared openly, it eliminates silos and promotes cross-functional cooperation. Employees are better equipped to understand how their work contributes to the broader organizational goals, leading to increased alignment and synergy. Collaboration becomes seamless as individuals have access to the necessary information and can make informed decisions.

Moreover, transparent communication helps to create a sense of belonging. When employees are aware of the company's vision, values, and goals, they can align their personal aspirations with the organization's mission. This alignment fosters a strong sense of purpose and encourages individuals to go the extra mile. Employees feel a greater sense of ownership and pride in their work, resulting in improved productivity and engagement.

In conclusion, the power of transparent communication cannot be underestimated. It is a vital component of organizational behavior that can transform workplaces and drive success. By fostering trust, collaboration, and a sense of belonging, transparent communication empowers individuals to become active contributors to their teams and organizations. As we delve deeper into this subchapter, we will explore practical strategies and tips for implementing transparent communication within your organization.

# Listening and Empathy: Keys to Effective Communication

In today's fast-paced world, effective communication has become increasingly important in all aspects of our lives, especially in the realm of organizational behavior. Whether you are a team leader, a manager, or a team member, the ability to communicate effectively can make a significant difference in the success of your team and the overall engagement of your employees. This subchapter will delve into the fundamental elements of effective communication: listening and empathy.

Listening is a skill that is often overlooked but is crucial to effective communication. It involves not only hearing the words being spoken but also understanding the underlying message and emotions conveyed. By actively listening, we show others that their words and opinions are valued, fostering a sense of trust and respect. Additionally, listening enables us to gather important information, perspectives, and insights that can help us make informed decisions and contribute to the overall success of our teams.

Empathy, on the other hand, is the ability to understand and share the feelings of others. It goes beyond sympathy and involves putting ourselves in someone else's shoes and truly experiencing their emotions. By practicing empathy, we can create a safe and supportive environment where individuals feel heard, understood, and validated. This, in turn, enhances teamwork, collaboration, and employee engagement.

To improve our listening and empathy skills, it is essential to be fully present in conversations. This means setting aside distractions, such as phones or other tasks, and giving our undivided attention to the person speaking. It also involves being open-minded and suspending judgment, allowing us to truly understand the perspective of others.

Furthermore, non-verbal cues play a significant role in effective communication. Paying attention to body language, facial expressions, and tone of voice can provide valuable insights into the emotions and intentions of the speaker. By being attuned to these cues, we can respond appropriately and demonstrate our empathy.

In conclusion, listening and empathy are the cornerstones of effective communication in organizational behavior. By honing these skills, we can build stronger teams, foster employee engagement, and create a positive and productive work environment. So, let us commit to actively listening and empathizing with others, and watch as our connections flourish and our teams thrive.

## Providing Feedback and Recognition

In any organization, one of the key drivers of success is the ability to provide effective feedback and recognition. The Power of Connection: Building Stronger Teams and Boosting Employee Engagement explores the crucial role that feedback and recognition play in enhancing organizational behavior. This subchapter delves into the importance of providing timely and constructive feedback, as well as the power of recognition in motivating and engaging employees.

Feedback is a vital tool for growth and development. It serves as a compass, guiding individuals and teams toward improvement. However, it is essential to provide feedback in a constructive and timely manner. Waiting too long to offer feedback can diminish its impact and leave employees feeling undervalued. By providing feedback regularly, managers and leaders can help individuals identify areas for improvement and celebrate their successes. This consistent feedback loop promotes a culture of continuous learning and growth within the organization.

Effective feedback should be specific, actionable, and focused on behavior rather than personal attributes. It is crucial to highlight both strengths and areas for improvement, as this balanced approach fosters a sense of trust and openness. Furthermore, feedback should be delivered in a respectful and empathetic manner, creating a safe environment for individuals to receive and process feedback.

Recognition is another powerful tool that drives employee engagement and organizational behavior. Acknowledging and appreciating employees' efforts and achievements not only boosts their morale but also reinforces positive behavior and performance. Recognition can take various forms, from a simple thank you note to public appreciation in team meetings or company-wide announcements. By recognizing and celebrating accomplishments, organizations create a culture of appreciation and motivate employees to go the extra mile.

In addition, recognizing and valuing diversity is crucial for building strong teams and boosting employee engagement. Embracing different perspectives and experiences fosters innovation and creativity, leading to improved problem-solving and decision-making within the organization. By actively seeking and appreciating diverse voices, organizations can create an inclusive environment that empowers individuals to contribute their unique skills and insights.

In conclusion, providing effective feedback and recognition is a cornerstone of organizational behavior. By offering timely and constructive feedback, organizations can guide individuals and teams towards growth and improvement. Moreover, recognizing and appreciating employees' efforts fosters a culture of engagement and motivation. By embracing diversity and valuing different perspectives, organizations can tap into the true potential of their teams. The Power of Connection: Building Stronger Teams and Boosting Employee Engagement provides practical insights and strategies for implementing feedback and recognition initiatives that enhance organizational behavior and drive success.

# Encouraging Two-Way Communication

In today's fast-paced and interconnected world, effective communication plays a crucial role in the success of any organization. It is the key to building stronger teams and boosting employee engagement. In this subchapter, we will explore the power of encouraging two-way communication within your organization and how it can positively impact the field of organizational behavior.

Two-way communication involves not only transmitting information from top to bottom but also creating an open and receptive environment where employees feel comfortable expressing their thoughts, ideas, and concerns. It promotes a culture of transparency, trust, and collaboration, leading to enhanced productivity and innovation.

One of the main benefits of two-way communication is that it empowers employees. When individuals feel valued and heard, they become more engaged in their work and are more likely to contribute their unique perspectives and skills. This, in turn, fosters a sense of ownership and accountability, creating a positive working atmosphere.

Moreover, two-way communication enables organizations to tap into the collective intelligence of their workforce. By actively seeking and listening to employee feedback, organizations can gain valuable insights into areas that need improvement, identify potential challenges, and create effective solutions. This not only enhances decision-making but also makes employees feel valued and respected, leading to higher job satisfaction and retention rates.

To encourage two-way communication, organizations can implement various strategies. First and foremost, leaders should lead by example and actively engage in open and honest communication with their teams. They should create opportunities for dialogue, such as regular team meetings, town halls, or suggestion boxes, where employees can freely express their opinions and concerns.

Additionally, technology can play a significant role in facilitating two-way communication. Utilizing digital platforms, such as email, instant messaging, or intranet forums, allows employees to provide feedback and share ideas in a non-threatening manner. Furthermore, organizations can establish mentorship programs or cross-functional teams to encourage collaboration and knowledge-sharing.

In conclusion, encouraging two-way communication is essential for organizations aiming to build stronger teams and boost employee engagement. By creating an environment where everyone's voice is heard and valued, organizations can tap into the collective intelligence of their workforce, improve decision-making, and drive innovation. Embracing this approach in the field of organizational behavior can revolutionize the way we work, fostering a culture of collaboration, trust, and growth for every individual.

# Leveraging Technology for Communication

In today's fast-paced and technology-driven world, effective communication is more crucial than ever before. Organizations have recognized the need to adapt and leverage technology to enhance communication processes and improve overall productivity. In this subchapter, we will explore the importance of leveraging technology for communication in the context of organizational behavior.

Technology has revolutionized the way we communicate, breaking down barriers of distance and time. With the click of a button, we can connect with colleagues, clients, and stakeholders from all corners of the globe. This instant connectivity has opened up a world of opportunities for organizations to collaborate, share information, and foster teamwork.

One of the key advantages of leveraging technology for communication is the ability to overcome geographical boundaries. With video conferencing tools, virtual meetings can be conducted, eliminating the need for travel and saving valuable time and resources. This level of connectivity allows teams to work together seamlessly, regardless of their physical location, leading to increased efficiency and productivity.

Moreover, technology facilitates real-time communication, enabling immediate feedback and response. Instant messaging platforms, such as Slack or Microsoft Teams, have become the go-to communication channels for organizations, replacing traditional email threads. This instant accessibility promotes faster decision-making, quick problem-solving, and enhances team collaboration.

Additionally, technology provides a platform for transparent and inclusive communication. Through intranet portals or project management tools, organizations can share information, updates, and important documents with the entire team. This transparency fosters a sense of trust and involvement, as everyone has access to the same information, eliminating any potential misunderstandings or miscommunication.

However, it is important to note that while technology can greatly enhance communication, it should not replace face-to-face interaction entirely. Effective communication involves not only the exchange of information but also the interpretation of non-verbal cues and building relationships. Therefore, organizations must strike a balance between leveraging technology for efficiency and maintaining meaningful interpersonal connections.

In conclusion, leveraging technology for communication is a powerful tool that can transform organizational behavior. It enables seamless collaboration, overcomes geographical barriers, promotes real-time feedback, and fosters transparency. However, organizations must remember that technology should complement, not replace, face-to-face interaction. By embracing technology and harnessing its capabilities, organizations can build stronger teams, boost employee engagement, and ultimately drive success in today's interconnected world.

# Chapter 4: Creating a Sense of Belonging and Connection

## Promoting Collaboration and Teamwork

In today's fast-paced and interconnected world, collaboration and teamwork have become essential for the success of any organization. In this subchapter, we will explore the power of collaboration and teamwork and how it can strengthen teams and boost employee engagement.

Collaboration is the process of working together towards a common goal. It involves pooling resources, sharing information, and leveraging the strengths and skills of team members. When individuals collaborate, they are able to accomplish more than what they could achieve individually. Collaboration also encourages creativity and innovation by bringing together diverse perspectives and ideas.

Teamwork, on the other hand, is the ability of a group of individuals to work together efficiently and effectively towards a shared objective. It requires open communication, trust, and a clear understanding of roles and responsibilities. Teamwork promotes a sense of unity and fosters a supportive and inclusive work environment.

To promote collaboration and teamwork within an organization, leaders must create a culture that encourages and rewards these behaviors. This can be done by establishing clear goals and objectives that are aligned with the organization's mission and values. Leaders should also provide the necessary resources and support for teams to collaborate effectively, such as training programs and collaboration tools.

Additionally, it is crucial to foster open communication and trust among team members. This can be achieved through regular team meetings, where individuals can share their ideas and concerns. Leaders should also encourage and recognize the contributions of each team member, promoting a sense of ownership and shared responsibility.

Moreover, organizations can benefit from promoting cross-functional collaboration, where individuals from different departments or areas of expertise come together to work on a project. This not only enhances knowledge-sharing but also breaks down silos and encourages a more holistic approach to problem-solving.

In conclusion, promoting collaboration and teamwork is vital for any organization's success. By fostering a culture of collaboration, leaders can build stronger teams and boost employee engagement. Collaboration encourages creativity, innovation, and efficiency, while teamwork creates a sense of unity and support within the organization. By implementing strategies to promote collaboration and teamwork, organizations can harness the power of connection and drive their success in today's competitive business landscape.

## Building Relationships and Trust

In today's fast-paced and ever-changing business landscape, building strong relationships and fostering trust among team members has become more crucial than ever. In this subchapter, we will explore the significance of building relationships and trust, and how it can enhance organizational behavior and boost employee engagement.

Relationships are the foundation of any successful team or organization. When team members have strong relationships with one another, they feel more connected, supported, and motivated to work towards common goals. Building relationships involves open communication, active listening, and genuine empathy. It requires investing time and effort in getting to know one another beyond just professional roles and responsibilities. By building strong relationships, teams can foster a sense of camaraderie, collaboration, and trust that is essential for achieving success.

Trust is the cornerstone of effective teamwork and organizational behavior. When trust exists among team members, it creates an environment where individuals feel safe to take risks, share ideas, and be vulnerable. Trust is built through consistent actions, reliability, and transparency. It requires leaders to lead by example, maintain confidentiality, and provide constructive feedback. Trust allows team members to rely on one another, delegate tasks, and work together seamlessly. It also minimizes conflicts and encourages open dialogue, leading to more efficient and productive outcomes.

Building relationships and trust not only strengthens teamwork but also boosts employee engagement. When employees feel connected to their colleagues and trust their leaders, they are more likely to be engaged and committed to their work. Engaged employees are motivated, enthusiastic, and willing to go the extra mile to achieve organizational goals. They have a sense of belonging and purpose, leading to increased productivity and overall satisfaction.

In conclusion, building relationships and trust is paramount in enhancing organizational behavior and boosting employee engagement. It requires effort, active listening, and a genuine commitment to fostering strong connections among team members. By prioritizing relationships and trust, organizations can create a positive work culture, improve teamwork, and ultimately achieve greater success. So, let's invest in building relationships and trust, and witness the power of connection in action.

# Celebrating Diversity and Inclusion

In today's rapidly changing world, organizations are increasingly recognizing the importance of diversity and inclusion. It is no longer enough to simply have a diverse workforce; organizations must create an inclusive environment where individuals from all backgrounds feel valued and empowered. This subchapter explores the significance of celebrating diversity and inclusion in the workplace and how it can lead to stronger teams and increased employee engagement.

Diversity is more than just differences in race, gender, or ethnicity; it encompasses a wide range of characteristics, such as age, religion, sexual orientation, and disability. Embracing diversity allows organizations to tap into a wealth of perspectives, experiences, and talents. It fosters creativity, innovation, and the ability to adapt to changing markets and customer needs. By celebrating diversity, organizations can also attract and retain top talent, as individuals are more likely to join organizations that embrace their unique qualities.

However, diversity alone is not enough. Inclusion is the key to unlocking the potential of a diverse workforce. Inclusive organizations create a sense of belonging, where all individuals feel respected, valued, and included in decision-making processes. Inclusion fosters collaboration, trust, and open communication, leading to stronger teams and higher employee engagement.

To celebrate diversity and promote inclusion, organizations can implement various strategies. This may include providing diversity and inclusion training to employees, creating employee resource groups and affinity networks, and establishing mentorship programs that connect individuals from different backgrounds. It is essential for organizations to promote a culture of inclusivity from the top-down, with leaders demonstrating their commitment to diversity and inclusion through their actions and behaviors.

By celebrating diversity and promoting inclusion, organizations can create a workplace where every individual can thrive. Employees are more likely to be engaged and motivated when they feel included and valued for who they are. This, in turn, leads to higher productivity, better decision-making, and ultimately, improved organizational performance.

In conclusion, celebrating diversity and inclusion is not only the right thing to do but also a strategic advantage for organizations. By embracing and valuing the differences among individuals, organizations can create stronger teams, boost employee engagement, and ultimately achieve greater success. It is time for organizations to recognize the power of diversity and inclusion and take proactive steps to ensure that everyone feels included and valued within their workplaces.

# Developing a Sense of Community

In today's fast-paced and ever-evolving corporate world, building a sense of community within organizations has become more important than ever. The Power of Connection: Building Stronger Teams and Boosting Employee Engagement explores the significance of developing a sense of community and its impact on organizational behavior.

Community, in the context of the workplace, refers to a group of individuals who share common values, goals, and aspirations. When employees feel a strong sense of community, they are more engaged, motivated, and committed to their work. This subchapter delves into the various ways in which organizations can foster a sense of community and improve overall employee satisfaction.

One of the key aspects of developing a sense of community is fostering open communication and collaboration. When employees feel comfortable expressing their ideas and opinions, it not only enhances their engagement but also encourages them to contribute actively to the organization's growth. This subchapter discusses effective communication strategies, such as regular team meetings, open-door policies, and the use of technology platforms for virtual collaboration.

Furthermore, building a sense of community also involves promoting a culture of inclusivity and diversity. Organizations that value and respect individual differences create an environment where employees feel a sense of belonging. The subchapter explores the importance of diversity and inclusion initiatives, such as employee resource groups, mentorship programs, and diversity training, in developing a strong community within the workplace.

Another vital aspect of fostering a sense of community is recognizing and celebrating achievements. By acknowledging and rewarding employees' hard work and accomplishments, organizations can boost morale and create a positive work environment. This subchapter highlights the significance of employee recognition programs and the role they play in strengthening the sense of community.

Lastly, the subchapter emphasizes the role of leadership in developing a sense of community. Leaders who demonstrate authenticity, empathy, and inclusivity are more likely to inspire and engage their teams. The subchapter provides practical tips for leaders to effectively build and sustain a sense of community within their organizations.

In conclusion, developing a sense of community is crucial for enhancing organizational behavior. By promoting open communication, embracing diversity and inclusion, recognizing achievements, and fostering effective leadership, organizations can create a strong sense of community that leads to increased employee engagement and overall success.

# Encouraging Social Connections

In today's fast-paced and highly competitive business world, organizations often overlook the importance of social connections in the workplace. However, fostering strong social connections among employees is crucial for building stronger teams and boosting overall employee engagement. This subchapter delves into the significance of encouraging social connections and provides practical strategies for creating a more connected and collaborative work environment.

Humans are social beings by nature. We thrive on social interactions and connections with others, and the workplace is no exception. Cultivating social connections within an organization not only enhances employee well-being but also has a direct impact on organizational behavior and performance.

One key benefit of encouraging social connections is the creation of a positive and inclusive work culture. When employees feel connected to their colleagues, they are more likely to collaborate, share ideas, and provide support to one another. This sense of camaraderie fosters a collaborative environment where individuals feel comfortable expressing their opinions and seeking help when needed. As a result, teams become more cohesive and efficient in achieving their goals.

Furthermore, social connections play a crucial role in employee engagement. When employees have strong social ties at work, they feel a sense of belonging and are more likely to be emotionally invested in their work. This, in turn, leads to higher levels of job satisfaction, productivity, and a decreased likelihood of turnover. Encouraging social connections can also help alleviate workplace stress and improve mental well-being, as employees feel supported and valued by their peers.

To foster social connections within your organization, it is essential to create opportunities for employees to interact and collaborate. This can be achieved through team-building activities, social events, or even simple initiatives like designated common areas for informal conversations. Encouraging cross-functional collaborations and promoting open communication channels also facilitate social connections among employees.

In addition, leveraging technology can be a powerful tool for enhancing social connections, especially in remote or distributed teams. Virtual platforms and social networking tools can facilitate communication, knowledge sharing, and relationship building, enabling employees to connect and engage with their colleagues irrespective of geographical locations.

In conclusion, encouraging social connections within the workplace is a crucial aspect of organizational behavior and employee engagement. By fostering a sense of community and creating opportunities for interaction, organizations can build stronger teams, enhance collaboration, and boost overall performance. Investing in social connections not only benefits employees' well-being but also contributes to the long-term success and growth of the organization as a whole.

# Chapter 5: Empowering Employees for Engagement

## Giving Autonomy and Ownership

In today's rapidly changing business landscape, organizations are increasingly recognizing the importance of giving autonomy and ownership to their employees. This subchapter delves into the significance of empowering individuals within teams and how it can drive higher engagement levels and promote a stronger sense of ownership among employees.

Autonomy is the ability for individuals to have control and independence in their work. It allows employees to make decisions and take ownership of their tasks, fostering a sense of responsibility and accountability. When individuals are given the freedom to exercise their judgment and creativity, it not only boosts their confidence but also enhances their overall job satisfaction.

Empowering employees with autonomy leads to a more engaged workforce. Studies have shown that when individuals feel trusted and have the freedom to work in their own way, they are more likely to be motivated, innovative, and committed to delivering high-quality results. Autonomy allows individuals to tailor their work to their strengths and preferences, resulting in increased job satisfaction and a sense of personal fulfillment.

Ownership, on the other hand, refers to the feeling of being responsible for the outcomes of one's work. When employees have a sense of ownership, they are more likely to go above and beyond their role, take initiative, and take pride in their contributions. This sense of ownership fosters a culture of accountability, where individuals are motivated to achieve their goals and strive for excellence.

To create a culture of autonomy and ownership, leaders must provide clear expectations and guidelines while allowing room for individuals to make decisions and contribute their unique perspectives. It is crucial to establish open lines of communication, where employees feel comfortable sharing their ideas, concerns, and suggestions. Leaders should also provide ongoing feedback and support to ensure individuals feel valued and empowered in their roles.

Moreover, organizations should invest in training and development programs that equip employees with the knowledge and skills necessary to confidently take ownership of their work. By fostering a learning culture and providing opportunities for growth, organizations can empower individuals to continually improve and take on new challenges.

In conclusion, giving autonomy and ownership to employees is crucial for building stronger teams and boosting employee engagement. It enables individuals to feel trusted, motivated, and responsible for their work, leading to increased job satisfaction and overall team success. By creating a culture that fosters autonomy and ownership, organizations can unleash the full potential of their employees and drive continuous growth and innovation.

# Providing Meaningful Work

## Subchapter: Providing Meaningful Work

In today's fast-paced and ever-changing work environment, organizations are recognizing the importance of providing employees with meaningful work. When employees feel that their work is purposeful and aligned with their values, it not only boosts their engagement and satisfaction but also leads to improved organizational performance. This subchapter delves into the significance of providing meaningful work and how it can positively impact organizational behavior.

Meaningful work goes beyond just completing tasks and meeting deadlines; it involves connecting employees with a larger purpose and making them feel that their contributions matter. When employees understand how their work fits into the bigger picture and how it impacts the organization and society as a whole, they are more likely to be motivated and engaged. They derive a sense of fulfillment and pride, which can lead to increased productivity and a stronger commitment to their roles.

One way to provide meaningful work is by clearly communicating the organization's mission, vision, and values. When employees are aware of the organization's purpose and understand how their work contributes to achieving those goals, they are more likely to find meaning in what they do. Regularly reminding employees of the organization's mission and recognizing their contributions towards it can help reinforce the sense of purpose and meaning in their work.

Another crucial aspect of providing meaningful work is offering opportunities for growth and development. Employees who feel stagnant and unchallenged are more likely to lose motivation and disengage. Organizations can foster a culture of continuous learning and growth by providing training programs, mentoring opportunities, and chances to take on new responsibilities. This not only helps employees develop their skills but also allows them to see the potential for advancement and personal growth within the organization.

Furthermore, involving employees in decision-making processes can contribute to the sense of meaningful work. When employees have a voice and are given the opportunity to contribute their ideas and opinions, they feel valued and recognized. This involvement can lead to a greater sense of ownership and commitment to the organization's goals, resulting in increased engagement and improved organizational behavior.

Providing meaningful work is not just a buzzword; it is a fundamental aspect of creating a positive work environment and promoting employee engagement. By aligning employees' work with a larger purpose, offering growth opportunities, and involving them in decision-making processes, organizations can build stronger teams and enhance overall organizational behavior. When employees feel that their work matters, they are more likely to bring their best selves to work and contribute to the success of the organization.

## Supporting Work-Life Balance

In today's fast-paced and demanding work environment, finding a healthy balance between work and personal life is crucial for overall well-being and productivity. Organizations that prioritize supporting work-life balance not only benefit their employees but also create a positive and engaging work culture. This subchapter aims to explore the importance of work-life balance and provide practical strategies that individuals and organizations can adopt to achieve it.

Work-life balance refers to the equilibrium between professional responsibilities and personal life commitments. It recognizes the need for individuals to have time and energy for their families, hobbies, self-care, and personal development outside of work. When work-life balance is achieved, employees experience reduced stress levels, increased job satisfaction, and improved mental and physical health. This, in turn, leads to higher engagement, productivity, and retention rates within organizations.

To support work-life balance, organizations can implement various initiatives. Firstly, flexible work arrangements, such as remote work options or flexible schedules, allow employees to better manage their personal commitments while fulfilling their work responsibilities. This flexibility empowers individuals to structure their work in a way that suits their unique needs, ultimately leading to better work-life integration.

Furthermore, organizations can encourage employees to prioritize self-care by promoting wellness programs. These programs can include activities like yoga or meditation classes, wellness challenges, or access to fitness facilities. By investing in their employees' well-being, organizations demonstrate their commitment to creating a healthy work environment that fosters work-life balance.

Additionally, effective communication plays a vital role in supporting work-life balance. Organizations can encourage open dialogue between managers and employees to ensure that expectations, goals, and deadlines are clear and realistic. Regular check-ins and feedback sessions can help identify and address any potential work-life conflicts, allowing for proactive solutions to be implemented.

Individuals also play a significant role in achieving work-life balance. By setting boundaries, managing time effectively, and prioritizing self-care, individuals can create a healthy integration between their professional and personal lives. Engaging in activities that promote relaxation and rejuvenation, such as spending quality time with loved ones, pursuing hobbies, or taking regular breaks, can significantly contribute to a balanced and fulfilling lifestyle.

In conclusion, supporting work-life balance is crucial for organizations to ensure the well-being and engagement of their employees. By implementing flexible work arrangements, wellness programs, and fostering effective communication, organizations can create an environment that promotes work-life balance. Simultaneously, individuals must take responsibility for managing their time effectively and prioritizing self-care. By striving for work-life balance, individuals and organizations can create stronger teams, boost employee engagement, and ultimately achieve greater success in both personal and professional spheres.

## Encouraging Innovation and Creativity

In today's fast-paced and ever-changing business landscape, organizations must foster a culture of innovation and creativity to stay competitive and drive growth. In this subchapter, we will explore the power of encouraging innovation and creativity within teams and how it can significantly boost employee engagement.

Innovation and creativity are essential for organizations seeking to adapt to new challenges, seize opportunities, and create breakthrough solutions. By embracing new ideas and approaches, companies can differentiate themselves from competitors, enhance customer satisfaction, and drive profitability. However, fostering innovation and creativity requires more than just providing resources; it demands a supportive environment that encourages employees to take risks, think outside the box, and experiment with new ideas.

One crucial factor in encouraging innovation and creativity is leadership. Leaders play a pivotal role in setting the tone and creating an atmosphere that nurtures innovative thinking. They must create an environment that promotes psychological safety, where employees feel comfortable sharing their ideas without fear of judgment or criticism. By fostering an open and non-judgmental culture, leaders can empower their teams to think creatively and explore new possibilities.

Another key element is providing employees with the necessary tools and resources to foster innovation. This includes investing in training programs that enhance creative thinking, providing access to cutting-edge technology, and creating platforms for collaboration and idea-sharing. By equipping employees with the right tools, organizations can empower them to unleash their creativity and drive innovation within their respective roles.

Furthermore, organizations should encourage diversity and inclusivity to foster innovation. By bringing together individuals with different backgrounds, experiences, and perspectives, organizations can tap into a wealth of creative ideas and innovative solutions. Embracing diversity not only enriches the creative process but also promotes a sense of belonging and engagement among employees.

Lastly, organizations should celebrate and recognize innovative thinking and creativity. By acknowledging and rewarding employees who generate impactful ideas, organizations show their commitment to fostering innovation. This recognition can take the form of monetary rewards, promotions, or even dedicating specific channels to showcase and implement employee ideas. Celebrating innovation not only boosts morale and engagement but also inspires others to think creatively and contribute to the organization's success.

In conclusion, encouraging innovation and creativity is vital for organizations looking to thrive in today's dynamic business environment. By fostering a culture that supports and celebrates innovative thinking, organizations can unlock the full potential of their employees and drive growth. Leaders must create an environment that promotes psychological safety, provide the necessary tools and resources, encourage diversity, and recognize and celebrate innovative ideas. By doing so, organizations can build stronger teams, boost employee engagement, and position themselves as leaders in their respective industries.

## Recognizing and Rewarding Contributions

In today's fast-paced and competitive work environment, recognizing and rewarding the contributions of employees has become more crucial than ever before. This subchapter aims to shed light on the importance of acknowledging the efforts and achievements of individuals within an organization, while also exploring effective strategies for rewarding these contributions.

Recognizing and rewarding contributions is a powerful tool for enhancing employee engagement and promoting a positive work culture. When employees feel appreciated and valued for their hard work, they are more likely to be motivated, productive, and loyal to the organization. Moreover, recognition can foster a sense of belonging and camaraderie among team members, thus strengthening interpersonal relationships and promoting collaboration.

Organizations can adopt various approaches to recognize and reward contributions effectively. One common method is through verbal praise and public acknowledgement. Managers and leaders should make a conscious effort to recognize employees' achievements publicly, whether it be during team meetings, company-wide emails, or even through social media platforms. By doing so, individuals are not only acknowledged for their efforts but also serve as role models for others to aspire to.

Another effective way to reward contributions is through incentive programs. These can range from monetary bonuses, gift cards, or even extra days off. These rewards provide tangible recognition for exceptional performance and can serve as powerful motivators for employees to continue excelling in their roles.

However, it is essential to remember that recognition and rewards should not be limited to monetary incentives alone. Non-financial rewards, such as flexible work hours, professional development opportunities, or even a simple handwritten note of appreciation, can have a significant impact on employees' motivation and job satisfaction.

To ensure the success of recognition and reward programs, organizations must also prioritize fairness and transparency. Employees should perceive the process as equitable and based on objective criteria, rather than favoritism or nepotism. Regular feedback and open lines of communication are essential in this regard, allowing employees to understand the expectations and criteria for recognition and reward.

In conclusion, recognizing and rewarding contributions is a vital aspect of organizational behavior. By implementing effective strategies to acknowledge and appreciate employees' efforts, organizations can boost employee engagement, promote a positive work culture, and ultimately achieve higher levels of productivity and success. It is crucial for every organization to prioritize recognizing and rewarding contributions to build stronger teams and foster a highly engaged workforce.

# Chapter 6: Developing Strong Leadership for Engagement

## The Role of Leaders in Employee Engagement

In today's rapidly changing business landscape, organizations are realizing the importance of employee engagement in driving success and achieving sustainable growth. Employee engagement refers to the level of commitment and enthusiasm employees have towards their work and the organization they belong to. It is a crucial factor that directly impacts productivity, innovation, and overall performance.

Leaders play a pivotal role in fostering employee engagement within an organization. They are responsible for setting the tone, creating a positive work environment, and inspiring their teams to achieve greatness. Effective leaders understand the significance of employee engagement and actively work towards cultivating it. They understand that engaged employees are more likely to go the extra mile, collaborate effectively, and stay loyal to the organization.

One of the primary roles of leaders in employee engagement is creating a strong sense of purpose and vision. Leaders must clearly communicate the organization's goals and objectives, ensuring employees understand how their work contributes to the bigger picture. By aligning individual and team goals with the organization's mission, leaders empower employees to feel a sense of purpose, which in turn fuels engagement.

Leaders also play a crucial role in providing regular feedback and recognition. Employees need to know that their efforts are valued and recognized. Leaders must offer constructive feedback, highlighting areas of improvement, and also acknowledge achievements and milestones. This not only boosts employee morale but also creates a culture of continuous growth and learning.

Furthermore, leaders must actively listen to their employees and address their concerns and needs. By fostering open communication channels, leaders can ensure that employees feel heard, valued, and supported. This can be achieved through regular team meetings, one-on-one discussions, and employee surveys. By actively seeking feedback and acting upon it, leaders can build trust and create an environment where employees feel safe to voice their opinions and ideas.

Lastly, leaders must lead by example. They must display the behaviors and values they expect from their team members. By embodying integrity, resilience, and a strong work ethic, leaders inspire their employees to do the same. Leaders who demonstrate a genuine passion and commitment towards their work create a contagious energy that motivates and engages their teams.

In conclusion, leaders have a crucial role in fostering employee engagement within an organization. By creating a strong sense of purpose, providing regular feedback and recognition, actively listening to employees, and leading by example, leaders can build a highly engaged workforce. Employee engagement is not a one-time task but rather an ongoing effort that requires continuous attention and nurturing. When leaders prioritize employee engagement, they create a work environment that fosters collaboration, innovation, and ultimately drives organizational success.

# Building Trust and Credibility as a Leader

Trust and credibility are essential qualities for effective leadership. In today's fast-paced and ever-changing business environment, leaders must be able to build and maintain trust with their teams to drive success. In this subchapter, we will explore the significance of trust and credibility, and provide practical tips for enhancing these qualities as a leader.

Trust is the foundation of any successful relationship, and this holds true in the workplace as well. When employees trust their leaders, they are more likely to be engaged, productive, and committed to the organization's goals. Trust empowers individuals to take risks, voice their opinions, and collaborate openly. As a leader, it is crucial to understand that trust is not automatically given; it must be earned.

One way to build trust and credibility is through effective communication. Open and honest communication fosters transparency and creates an environment where employees feel valued and respected. Leaders should actively listen to their team members, provide constructive feedback, and be transparent about their own goals and expectations. By communicating with authenticity and empathy, leaders can forge strong connections and build trust.

Another important aspect of building trust and credibility is setting a positive example. Leaders should demonstrate integrity, consistency, and accountability in their actions. When leaders consistently follow through on their promises and uphold ethical standards, they establish a culture of trust within the organization. By leading by example, leaders inspire their teams to do the same.

Building trust also requires recognizing and valuing individual strengths and contributions. Leaders should empower their employees by delegating responsibilities, providing growth opportunities, and acknowledging achievements. By showing genuine appreciation and recognizing the unique contributions of each team member, leaders can create a sense of trust and belonging.

In addition to trust, credibility is crucial for effective leadership. Credibility is built on a foundation of expertise, competence, and reliability. Leaders must continuously develop their skills and knowledge to stay relevant in their field. By staying up-to-date with industry trends and seeking professional development opportunities, leaders can enhance their credibility and gain the respect of their teams.

To summarize, building trust and credibility as a leader is essential for fostering strong teams and boosting employee engagement. By prioritizing effective communication, leading by example, recognizing individual contributions, and continuously developing their skills, leaders can cultivate trust and credibility within their organizations. Remember, trust is earned over time, and it requires consistent effort and actions. As a leader, investing in building trust and credibility will yield long-term benefits for both individuals and the organization as a whole.

# Effective Communication for Leadership Engagement

In the dynamic and ever-evolving world of business, effective communication lies at the heart of successful leadership engagement. Whether you are a seasoned executive, a team lead, or an aspiring manager, the ability to communicate clearly and persuasively is crucial for building stronger teams and boosting employee engagement. This subchapter explores the power of effective communication and provides practical strategies for leaders to enhance their communication skills.

Effective communication begins with active listening. As a leader, it is essential to understand the needs, concerns, and aspirations of your team members. By actively listening to their ideas, suggestions, and feedback, you create an environment where individuals feel valued and understood. This fosters trust and promotes open dialogue, enabling you to create an engaged and motivated workforce.

Furthermore, leaders must master the art of being concise and articulate. In today's fast-paced world, attention spans are shorter than ever. By delivering clear and concise messages, leaders ensure that their ideas are understood and remembered by their teams. Avoiding jargon and using simple language helps to eliminate confusion, making communication more effective and impactful.

Another vital aspect of effective communication is the ability to adapt your style to different individuals and situations. Every person has a unique communication style, and understanding and adapting to these differences is key to effective leadership engagement. Some team members may prefer face-to-face interactions, while others may prefer written communication. By adapting your approach, you can establish stronger connections and engage individuals more effectively.

In addition to adapting your style, leaders must also consider non-verbal communication. Body language, facial expressions, and tone of voice can convey powerful messages that words alone cannot. Being aware of your own non-verbal cues and paying attention to those of others can improve understanding and prevent miscommunication.

Finally, leaders must embrace the power of storytelling. Stories have a remarkable ability to captivate and inspire, making them a powerful tool for engaging employees. By sharing compelling stories that resonate with your team members, you can create an emotional connection that motivates and inspires them to perform at their best.

In conclusion, effective communication is a vital skill for leaders in any organization. By practicing active listening, being concise and articulate, adapting to different styles, considering non-verbal cues, and utilizing storytelling, leaders can enhance their communication skills and engage their teams more effectively. By building stronger connections and boosting employee engagement, leaders can ultimately drive success and create a positive organizational culture.

# Empowering and Developing Employees as a Leader

Introduction:

In today's rapidly changing business landscape, effective leadership is no longer just about commanding and controlling. It is about empowering and developing employees to reach their full potential. This subchapter explores the importance of empowering and developing employees as a leader, and how it can contribute to building stronger teams and boosting employee engagement. Whether you are a CEO, manager, or team leader, the principles discussed here will help you create a positive and productive work environment.

Understanding Empowerment:

Empowerment is the process of giving employees the authority, autonomy, and resources to make decisions and take ownership of their work. It is about fostering a sense of trust, respect, and accountability within the organization. By empowering employees, leaders can tap into their unique talents, ideas, and perspectives, leading to increased innovation, productivity, and job satisfaction.

Developing Employees:

Employee development is an ongoing process that focuses on enhancing skills, knowledge, and abilities. As a leader, it is crucial to invest in your employees' development, as it not only benefits them individually but also contributes to the overall success of the organization. From providing training and mentoring opportunities to creating a culture of continuous learning, developing employees should be a top priority for every leader.

Benefits of Empowering and Developing Employees:

1. Increased Engagement: Empowered and developed employees are more engaged in their work, resulting in higher levels of commitment, motivation, and productivity.

2. Improved Problem-Solving: When employees are empowered to make decisions, they become more proactive and creative in finding solutions to challenges.

3. Enhanced Team Performance: Empowering and developing employees fosters a collaborative and supportive work environment, leading to better teamwork and cohesion.

4. Talent Retention: Employees who feel valued and supported are more likely to stay with the organization, reducing turnover and recruitment costs.

5. Organizational Growth: By empowering and developing employees, leaders can unlock the full potential of their workforce, leading to increased innovation and competitive advantage.

Conclusion:

Empowering and developing employees is not only beneficial for individual employees but also crucial for the success of the organization. By embracing these principles, leaders can create a culture of trust, collaboration, and continuous learning, resulting in stronger teams and higher levels of employee engagement. Whether you are a CEO, manager, or team leader, investing in your employees' empowerment and development will undoubtedly yield long-term benefits for both the individuals and the organization as a whole.

# Leading by Example: Modeling Engagement

In the realm of organizational behavior, one key aspect that has the power to transform teams and boost employee engagement is the ability of leaders to lead by example. This subchapter explores the significance of modeling engagement and how it can inspire and motivate individuals within an organization.

Leadership is not merely about holding a position of authority; it is about guiding and inspiring others towards a common goal. When leaders themselves exhibit high levels of engagement, it sets the tone for the entire organization. By modeling the behavior they wish to see in their teams, leaders can create a ripple effect that spreads enthusiasm and commitment throughout the workplace.

Leading by example encompasses various facets of engagement, starting with passion. Passionate leaders are not only driven by their own zeal but also have the ability to ignite the same fire in their teams. They demonstrate genuine excitement for the work they do, and this enthusiasm becomes contagious, inspiring others to invest their energy and creativity into their roles.

Another vital aspect of modeling engagement is embracing a growth mindset. Leaders who exhibit a willingness to learn, adapt, and improve create an environment that encourages continuous development. By demonstrating their own commitment to growth, leaders motivate their teams to seek out opportunities for learning and strive for excellence.

Transparency is yet another crucial element of leading by example. When leaders openly communicate with their teams, sharing both successes and failures, it fosters trust and openness within the organization. This transparency not only encourages employees to be more engaged but also empowers them to take ownership of their work and contribute to the overall success of the team.

Finally, leaders who prioritize work-life balance and self-care demonstrate the importance of taking care of oneself to maintain optimal engagement. By setting boundaries and encouraging their teams to do the same, leaders promote a healthy and sustainable work environment where employee well-being is valued.

In conclusion, leaders who model engagement have the power to transform organizational behavior and boost employee engagement. Through their passion, growth mindset, transparency, and focus on well-being, leaders inspire and motivate their teams to be fully engaged in their work. By leading by example, leaders create a positive and productive workplace culture that fosters collaboration, innovation, and ultimately, organizational success.

# Chapter 7: Sustaining and Measuring Employee Engagement

## Creating a Continuous Improvement Culture

In today's fast-paced and competitive business environment, organizations are constantly seeking ways to improve their performance, increase productivity, and stay ahead of the curve. One of the most effective strategies to achieve this is by creating a continuous improvement culture within the company. By fostering an environment that encourages learning, growth, and innovation, organizations can empower their employees to strive for excellence and drive positive change.

A continuous improvement culture is based on the belief that there is always room for improvement and that every individual has the potential to contribute to the betterment of the organization. It is about creating a mindset where employees are encouraged to question the status quo, identify opportunities for improvement, and take ownership of their work. This subchapter of "The Power of Connection: Building Stronger Teams and Boosting Employee Engagement" explores the key elements and best practices for creating a continuous improvement culture within any organization.

First and foremost, it is essential to establish a clear vision and purpose that aligns with the organization's goals. This vision should emphasize the importance of continuous improvement and set high standards for performance. By clearly communicating this vision to every member of the organization, leaders can create a sense of purpose and direction that motivates employees to actively seek ways to improve.

Moreover, fostering a culture of trust and psychological safety is crucial for encouraging employees to share their ideas and take risks. When individuals feel safe to voice their opinions and propose new ideas without fear of judgment or criticism, they are more likely to contribute to the organization's improvement initiatives. Creating opportunities for open and honest communication, such as regular feedback sessions and idea-sharing platforms, can help build trust and encourage collaboration.

To further enhance the continuous improvement culture, organizations should invest in ongoing learning and development opportunities. Providing employees with access to training programs, workshops, and mentorship can equip them with the necessary skills and knowledge to identify improvement opportunities and implement effective solutions. Additionally, recognizing and rewarding individuals and teams for their contributions towards continuous improvement can reinforce the desired behaviors and motivate others to follow suit.

In conclusion, creating a continuous improvement culture is a vital aspect of organizational behavior that can significantly enhance performance and employee engagement. By fostering an environment that values learning, innovation, and collaboration, organizations can empower their employees to actively contribute to the organization's success. Through a clear vision, trust, ongoing learning, and recognition, organizations can build a culture where continuous improvement becomes ingrained in the DNA of the company, leading to increased productivity, innovation, and success.

# Conducting Regular Employee Engagement Surveys

Employee engagement is a vital aspect of any organization's success. When employees are engaged, they are motivated, productive, and committed to achieving the organization's goals. Conducting regular employee engagement surveys is an effective tool to measure and improve engagement levels within an organization. In this chapter, we will explore the importance of conducting these surveys and how they can benefit both employees and the organization as a whole.

Regular employee engagement surveys provide valuable insights into the overall satisfaction and engagement levels of employees. They allow organizations to identify areas of strength and areas that need improvement. By collecting feedback from employees, organizations can gain a better understanding of what factors contribute to engagement and what factors may be hindering it. This information can then be used to develop targeted strategies to enhance employee engagement.

One of the key benefits of conducting regular employee engagement surveys is that it gives employees a voice. It allows them to express their opinions, concerns, and suggestions in a safe and anonymous manner. This, in turn, fosters a culture of open communication and trust within the organization. Employees feel valued and heard, which leads to increased job satisfaction and a stronger sense of belonging.

Moreover, these surveys provide organizations with the opportunity to benchmark their engagement levels against industry standards. By comparing their results with other organizations in the same industry, they can identify areas where they are performing well and areas where they need improvement. This benchmarking process helps organizations set realistic goals and measure their progress over time.

Conducting regular employee engagement surveys also demonstrates a commitment to continuous improvement. When employees see that their feedback is being actively sought and acted upon, they are more likely to feel engaged and motivated. It creates a sense of ownership and accountability among employees, as they know their opinions matter and can drive positive change within the organization.

In conclusion, conducting regular employee engagement surveys is a critical component of building stronger teams and boosting employee engagement. By listening to the voices of employees, organizations can identify areas for improvement, foster open communication, and demonstrate a commitment to continuous improvement. These surveys not only benefit employees by creating a more engaging work environment but also benefit the organization as a whole by increasing productivity, reducing turnover, and driving overall success.

# Analyzing and Acting on Employee Feedback

In today's rapidly evolving business landscape, organizations must prioritize employee feedback as a valuable tool for growth and success. Employee feedback serves as a powerful catalyst for change, enabling organizations to identify strengths, weaknesses, and areas for improvement. This subchapter delves into the importance of analyzing and acting on employee feedback, providing practical strategies to boost employee engagement and enhance organizational behavior.

Understanding the significance of employee feedback is crucial for every individual within an organization, regardless of their role or level. By actively seeking and valuing feedback, organizations foster a culture of open communication and transparency, which in turn promotes trust and collaboration. Employees who feel their voices are heard are more likely to be engaged and motivated, leading to higher productivity and overall organizational success.

Analyzing employee feedback is not merely about collecting data but rather gaining insights that can drive meaningful change. It involves a systematic approach to evaluate feedback, identify patterns, and discern underlying issues. By analyzing feedback, organizations can identify areas of improvement, address employee concerns, and implement changes that align with the organization's mission and values.

Acting on employee feedback is equally important, as it demonstrates a commitment to employee growth and well-being. This subchapter provides practical guidance on how to effectively act on feedback, such as creating action plans, involving employees in decision-making processes, and providing timely and constructive feedback. It emphasizes the need for accountability and follow-through to ensure that employee feedback is not disregarded but rather used to drive positive change.

Furthermore, this subchapter explores the impact of employee feedback on organizational behavior. It highlights how feedback can shape employee attitudes, behaviors, and interactions within the workplace. By addressing employee concerns and implementing changes based on feedback, organizations can foster a positive work environment that encourages collaboration, innovation, and growth.

In conclusion, analyzing and acting on employee feedback is a critical component of building stronger teams and boosting employee engagement. By valuing feedback, organizations can create a culture of trust, open communication, and continuous improvement. This subchapter equips individuals from various backgrounds and roles with practical strategies to effectively analyze and act on employee feedback, ultimately enhancing organizational behavior and driving success.

# Implementing Engagement Initiatives and Programs

In today's fast-paced and ever-changing business landscape, organizations are recognizing the importance of employee engagement as a critical driver of success. Engaged employees are not only more productive and motivated, but they also contribute to a positive work environment and foster a strong sense of commitment to the organization's goals and objectives. To harness the power of employee engagement, organizations must implement effective initiatives and programs that foster connection and a sense of belonging among their workforce.

This subchapter explores the various strategies and approaches organizations can employ to implement engagement initiatives and programs successfully. By focusing on organizational behavior, it provides valuable insights into the principles and practices that create an engaged and high-performing workforce.

One of the key aspects of implementing engagement initiatives is to create a culture of open communication and feedback. Organizations should encourage transparent and two-way communication channels that allow employees to express their opinions, ideas, and concerns freely. This fosters a sense of inclusion and makes employees feel valued, leading to increased engagement and job satisfaction.

Another essential element is the creation of meaningful and challenging work opportunities. By aligning employees' skills and interests with their roles and responsibilities, organizations can ensure that employees feel connected to their work and see the value they bring to the organization. This can be achieved through job enrichment, providing growth opportunities, and recognizing and rewarding employees' achievements.

Furthermore, organizations should invest in training and development programs that enhance employees' skills and competencies. By providing continuous learning opportunities, organizations not only enable employees to grow professionally but also demonstrate their commitment to employees' long-term success and growth.

In addition, implementing initiatives that promote work-life balance is crucial in today's fast-paced and demanding work environments. Organizations can introduce flexible work arrangements, wellness programs, and stress management initiatives to help employees maintain a healthy work-life balance, leading to increased engagement and overall well-being.

Finally, organizations should measure and track employee engagement levels regularly. Through surveys, feedback mechanisms, and performance evaluations, organizations can identify areas of improvement and assess the effectiveness of their engagement initiatives. This data-driven approach enables organizations to make informed decisions and continuously improve their engagement programs.

By implementing effective engagement initiatives and programs, organizations can build stronger teams, boost employee engagement, and create a positive work environment. This subchapter provides valuable insights and practical strategies to help organizations foster a culture of engagement and reap the benefits of a highly engaged workforce. Whether you are a business leader, manager, or an employee, this subchapter equips you with the knowledge and tools to enhance organizational behavior and drive success through employee engagement.

## Monitoring Progress and Celebrating Success

In any organization, it is crucial to regularly monitor progress and celebrate success. This subchapter explores the importance of tracking the progress of teams and individuals, and how acknowledging achievements can boost employee engagement and overall team morale.

Monitoring progress provides valuable insights into the effectiveness of current strategies and allows for timely adjustments if needed. It allows leaders to identify areas of improvement and recognize potential roadblocks before they become significant issues. By regularly evaluating progress, teams can stay on track and ensure that they are working towards their goals efficiently.

One effective method of monitoring progress is through the use of key performance indicators (KPIs). KPIs provide measurable targets that can be tracked and analyzed over time. By setting clear and realistic KPIs, individuals and teams can assess their performance objectively and identify areas for improvement. Regularly reviewing KPIs also provides an opportunity to celebrate milestones and achievements along the way.

Celebrating success is equally important as monitoring progress. Recognizing and rewarding accomplishments not only motivates individuals but also fosters a positive and supportive work culture. When achievements are celebrated, employees feel valued and appreciated for their hard work and dedication. This, in turn, boosts their confidence and encourages them to continue striving for excellence.

There are numerous ways to celebrate success within an organization. Publicly acknowledging and appreciating individuals or teams through announcements, emails, or company-wide meetings can help to create a sense of pride and camaraderie. Offering incentives such as bonuses, promotions, or additional time off can further reinforce the culture of success and motivate employees to go above and beyond.

Furthermore, celebrating success should not be limited to major milestones or exceptional achievements. Recognizing small wins and incremental progress is equally important. By acknowledging the efforts and progress made by individuals and teams, leaders can foster a sense of accomplishment and encourage continuous improvement.

In conclusion, monitoring progress and celebrating success are critical components of building stronger teams and boosting employee engagement. By regularly evaluating progress and acknowledging achievements, organizations can create a culture of success, where individuals are motivated to excel and contribute to the overall goals of the organization. Monitoring progress and celebrating success should be an ongoing practice that is embedded within the organizational behavior to ensure continued growth and success.

# Chapter 8: Overcoming Challenges to Employee Engagement

## Dealing with Resistance to Change

Change is an inevitable part of life, and this holds true for organizations as well. In today's rapidly evolving business landscape, organizations must be agile and adaptive to stay competitive. However, resistance to change is a common challenge that can hinder progress and innovation. In this subchapter, we will explore the concept of resistance to change and provide practical strategies for overcoming it, thereby fostering a culture of continuous improvement.

Resistance to change can manifest in various ways, including skepticism, fear, and reluctance. People often resist change because they fear the unknown, worry about their job security, or simply prefer the comfort of the familiar. However, effective leaders understand that change is necessary for growth and success, and they play a crucial role in managing resistance.

The first step in dealing with resistance to change is to communicate openly and transparently. When employees understand the reasons behind the change and how it will benefit the organization and themselves, they are more likely to embrace it. Leaders should take the time to address concerns, answer questions, and provide clarity throughout the change process. This open communication helps to alleviate fears and build trust.

Another important strategy is to involve employees in the change process. By including them in decision-making and seeking their input, leaders can empower employees and make them feel valued. This sense of ownership can significantly reduce resistance and increase engagement. Additionally, leaders should provide the necessary training and support to help employees adapt to the changes effectively. When employees have the knowledge and skills they need, they are more likely to embrace change with confidence.

Furthermore, leaders must lead by example. When leaders demonstrate a positive attitude towards change and actively participate in the transformation, they inspire their teams to do the same. It is essential to celebrate small wins along the way, acknowledge the efforts of individuals, and highlight success stories. This recognition reinforces the idea that change can be positive and encourages further engagement.

In conclusion, dealing with resistance to change is a critical aspect of organizational behavior. By communicating openly, involving employees, providing support, and leading by example, leaders can effectively manage resistance and create a culture that embraces change. Organizations that successfully navigate resistance to change are more likely to stay ahead of the curve, build stronger teams, and boost employee engagement. Remember, change may be challenging, but it also presents opportunities for growth and transformation.

## Addressing Burnout and Workload Issues

In today's fast-paced and demanding work environment, burnout and workload issues have become increasingly prevalent. Organizations across all industries are grappling with the negative consequences of these challenges, including decreased productivity, increased employee turnover, and diminished employee engagement. It is crucial for individuals and organizations to address these issues head-on in order to build stronger teams and boost employee engagement.

Burnout, often described as physical and emotional exhaustion, is a result of chronic workplace stress. It can manifest in various ways, such as decreased motivation, increased cynicism, and reduced job satisfaction. To combat burnout, individuals must prioritize self-care and establish healthy work-life boundaries. This includes setting realistic expectations, taking regular breaks, and seeking support from colleagues and managers. Organizations should also play a crucial role in creating a positive work environment that encourages work-life balance, stress management programs, and open communication channels.

Workload issues are another significant concern in organizational behavior. When employees are overloaded with tasks and responsibilities, they often feel overwhelmed and struggle to meet expectations. This can lead to decreased job satisfaction, compromised quality of work, and increased stress levels. Organizations need to adopt strategies to address workload issues, such as reevaluating job roles and responsibilities, redistributing tasks, and investing in automation and technology to streamline processes. Managers should regularly assess and adjust workloads to ensure they are reasonable and manageable.

Furthermore, it is essential for organizations to promote a culture of collaboration and support. Encouraging teamwork and providing opportunities for employees to share their workload and responsibilities can alleviate stress and prevent burnout. Leaders should prioritize open and transparent communication, allowing employees to voice their concerns and suggest improvements. By fostering a culture of trust and support, organizations can create an environment where individuals feel valued and appreciated, ultimately boosting employee engagement and overall team performance.

In conclusion, addressing burnout and workload issues is crucial for organizational success and employee well-being. By prioritizing self-care, establishing work-life boundaries, and implementing strategies to manage workloads effectively, organizations can create a positive work environment that fosters employee engagement. It is essential for both individuals and organizations to work together to address these challenges and build stronger teams.

## Managing Conflict and Difficult Employees

Conflict is an inevitable part of any organization, and managing it effectively is crucial for maintaining a harmonious work environment. In addition, dealing with difficult employees can pose a significant challenge for leaders and managers. This subchapter focuses on providing practical strategies for managing conflict and handling difficult employees, aimed at enhancing organizational behavior and promoting employee engagement.

Conflict within an organization can arise due to various reasons, such as differences in opinions, conflicting goals, or interpersonal issues. However, when managed properly, conflict can lead to positive outcomes, such as increased creativity, improved decision-making, and enhanced team dynamics. One effective approach to managing conflict is through open communication and active listening. Encouraging employees to express their concerns and viewpoints can help in resolving conflicts and finding mutually beneficial solutions. Additionally, fostering a culture of respect and empathy can create a safe space for employees to voice their opinions without fear of judgment or retaliation.

Dealing with difficult employees requires a different set of skills and strategies. It is essential to approach such employees with compassion and understanding, while also setting clear expectations and boundaries. Identifying the root causes of their behavior, such as personal issues or job-related frustrations, can provide insights into finding appropriate solutions. Implementing performance improvement plans, providing coaching and mentoring, or offering additional resources can help in addressing the underlying issues and supporting the employee's growth.

Furthermore, it is crucial for leaders and managers to remain objective and unbiased when dealing with conflict and difficult employees. Treating all employees fairly and consistently can help in maintaining trust and credibility. Implementing conflict resolution procedures and policies, such as mediation or arbitration, can also provide a structured framework for resolving conflicts professionally and impartially.

By effectively managing conflict and handling difficult employees, organizations can foster a positive work environment that promotes employee engagement and boosts overall productivity. Leaders and managers play a pivotal role in creating a culture that values open communication, respect, and empathy. When conflicts are managed constructively, and difficult employees are supported and guided, the entire organization benefits.

In conclusion, this subchapter serves as a valuable resource for individuals interested in organizational behavior and provides practical strategies for managing conflict and handling difficult employees. By implementing these strategies, organizations can strengthen their teams, improve employee engagement, and create a more positive and productive work environment.

# Navigating Organizational Politics

In the dynamic world of organizations, understanding and effectively navigating organizational politics is crucial for success. Organizational politics refers to the informal, often unwritten rules and power dynamics that influence decision-making, resource allocation, and career advancement within a company. It can be a complex and sometimes murky landscape to navigate, but with the right knowledge and skills, individuals can maneuver through it to achieve their goals and contribute to the success of their teams.

In this subchapter, we will explore the concept of organizational politics and provide practical strategies for effectively navigating it. Whether you are a seasoned professional or just starting out in your career, the insights shared here will empower you to navigate and leverage organizational politics to your advantage.

We will delve into the various dynamics that shape organizational politics, such as power structures, influence tactics, and networking. Understanding these dynamics will enable you to identify key players, power bases, and informal networks within your organization. By recognizing these factors, you can strategically align yourself with influential individuals and build strong alliances to enhance your influence and achieve your objectives.

Additionally, we will discuss the importance of ethical behavior in navigating organizational politics. While politics can sometimes be associated with negative connotations, it is possible to engage in politics ethically and with integrity. We will explore how to maintain your values and ethics while still being politically savvy, ensuring that your actions contribute positively to the overall organizational culture.

Furthermore, we will provide practical tips for building your political acumen, such as developing your emotional intelligence, enhancing your communication skills, and fostering a strong personal brand. These skills are essential for effectively navigating organizational politics and building strong relationships with colleagues and superiors.

By mastering the art of navigating organizational politics, you will be better equipped to influence decision-making, access resources, and advance your career. Moreover, you will be able to contribute to a positive and collaborative organizational culture, fostering employee engagement and stronger teams.

Whether you are an entry-level employee, a mid-level manager, or a senior executive, the insights shared in this subchapter will equip you with the knowledge and skills needed to navigate the intricate world of organizational politics. By harnessing the power of connection and understanding the dynamics at play, you will be able to build stronger teams, boost employee engagement, and ultimately drive success within your organization.

# Overcoming Remote Work Challenges

In today's digital age, remote work has become increasingly common, providing numerous benefits for both employees and employers. However, it also presents unique challenges that can hinder team collaboration and employee engagement. Understanding and overcoming these challenges is crucial to building stronger teams and boosting employee productivity. This subchapter explores some of the common obstacles faced in remote work and provides strategies to overcome them.

One of the primary challenges of remote work is the lack of face-to-face interaction, which can lead to feelings of isolation and disconnection. To overcome this, organizations should prioritize regular virtual meetings, encouraging team members to engage in video conferences rather than relying solely on emails or instant messaging. This helps foster a sense of camaraderie and allows for more effective communication.

Another challenge is maintaining work-life balance. Working from home can blur the boundaries between personal and professional life, leading to burnout and decreased productivity. To address this, individuals should establish a dedicated workspace and set clear boundaries between work and personal time. Employers can also support their remote employees by promoting flexible schedules and encouraging breaks throughout the day.

Effective communication is vital in remote work, but it can be hindered by technological barriers and time zone differences. Organizations should provide the necessary tools and resources for seamless communication, such as project management software and video conferencing platforms. It is also essential to establish clear communication guidelines, including response time expectations and preferred communication channels, to ensure everyone is on the same page.

Building trust within remote teams can be challenging, as there are limited opportunities for spontaneous interactions and team bonding. Employers can overcome this by implementing team-building activities, such as virtual happy hours or online games. Encouraging open and transparent communication also helps create a culture of trust and collaboration.

Finally, remote work can sometimes lead to a lack of accountability and productivity. To address this, organizations should establish clear goals and expectations, regularly track progress, and provide constructive feedback. Encouraging self-discipline and time management skills among remote employees is also crucial for maintaining productivity.

In conclusion, while remote work offers numerous benefits, it also presents unique challenges that need to be addressed to ensure strong teams and high employee engagement. By prioritizing effective communication, fostering work-life balance, building trust, and promoting accountability, organizations can overcome these challenges and reap the rewards of remote work.

# Chapter 9: The Future of Employee Engagement

## Trends and Innovations in Employee Engagement

In today's fast-paced and ever-evolving business landscape, organizations are constantly seeking ways to enhance employee engagement and build stronger teams. As the workforce becomes more diverse and technology continues to reshape the way we work, it is crucial for companies to stay ahead of the curve. This subchapter explores the latest trends and innovations in employee engagement, providing valuable insights for individuals and organizations alike.

One of the notable trends in employee engagement is the shift towards a more holistic approach. Gone are the days of focusing solely on monetary incentives and rewards. Organizations are now recognizing the importance of fostering a sense of purpose and meaning in employees' work. This can be achieved by aligning company values with individual goals, promoting work-life balance, and providing opportunities for personal and professional growth.

Another emerging trend is the use of technology to enhance employee engagement. With the rise of remote work and the increasing reliance on digital communication tools, companies are finding innovative ways to connect and engage with their employees. From virtual team-building activities to online learning platforms, technology offers a multitude of opportunities to foster collaboration, boost morale, and create a sense of belonging.

Additionally, companies are leveraging data and analytics to measure and improve employee engagement. By collecting and analyzing data on employee satisfaction, feedback, and performance, organizations can identify areas of improvement and implement targeted strategies.

This data-driven approach allows for a more personalized and effective engagement strategy, benefiting both employees and the overall organizational culture.

Furthermore, the subchapter explores the growing focus on employee well-being. As awareness around mental health and wellness increases, companies are prioritizing initiatives that support their employees' physical, emotional, and mental well-being. This includes offering flexible work arrangements, providing access to wellness programs, and promoting a healthy work-life balance. By prioritizing employee well-being, organizations not only improve engagement but also create a more positive and inclusive work environment.

In conclusion, the trends and innovations in employee engagement are constantly evolving to meet the needs of today's workforce. By adopting a holistic approach, leveraging technology, utilizing data and analytics, and prioritizing employee well-being, organizations can build stronger teams and boost employee engagement. Whether you are an individual looking to enhance your own engagement or an organization seeking to improve your team dynamics, this subchapter provides valuable insights and practical strategies to help you thrive in the ever-changing world of organizational behavior.

## Adapting to a Changing Workforce

In today's fast-paced and ever-evolving world, organizations must learn to adapt to a changing workforce. The dynamics of the modern workplace are shifting, and businesses need to stay ahead of the game to remain competitive. This subchapter explores the importance of embracing change and provides practical strategies for organizations to navigate the complexities of the changing workforce.

One of the key factors contributing to the changing workforce is the rise of technology. With advancements in automation, artificial intelligence, and remote work options, traditional job roles are being transformed. Organizations need to embrace these technological changes and equip their employees with the necessary skills to thrive in this digital era.

Another significant factor shaping the workforce is the increasing diversity in the workplace. Companies are becoming more multicultural, with employees from various backgrounds, ages, and experiences. Embracing diversity is not only essential for fostering an inclusive work environment but also for enhancing creativity, innovation, and problem-solving. Organizations must implement diversity and inclusion initiatives that promote equality and respect for all employees.

Furthermore, the gig economy has gained momentum, with an increasing number of workers opting for freelance or contract-based employment. This trend presents both opportunities and challenges for organizations. On one hand, it allows for greater flexibility and access to specialized skills. On the other hand, it requires organizations to rethink their traditional employment models and find ways to engage and retain gig workers effectively.

To adapt to these changes, organizations must focus on creating a culture of continuous learning and development. Employees need to be equipped with the skills and knowledge required to navigate the evolving workplace. This can be achieved through training programs, mentorship opportunities, and fostering a growth mindset within the organization.

Additionally, organizations should invest in technology that enables remote collaboration and communication. With the rise of remote work, teams are becoming more geographically dispersed. Providing employees with the tools and resources to effectively collaborate, regardless of their physical location, is crucial for maintaining productivity and engagement.

In conclusion, adapting to a changing workforce is crucial for organizations to stay relevant and competitive in today's world. By embracing technological advancements, fostering diversity and inclusion, and creating a culture of continuous learning, organizations can navigate the complexities of the modern workplace. The ability to adapt will not only attract and retain top talent but also boost employee engagement and drive business success.

# Embracing Technology for Engagement

In today's fast-paced and interconnected world, technology is playing an increasingly vital role in our daily lives. From communication to productivity, technology has revolutionized the way we work and interact with one another. As such, it is crucial that organizations harness the power of technology to enhance employee engagement and foster stronger teams.

Technology has the ability to break down barriers and bridge gaps in communication, enabling employees to connect with one another regardless of time zones or geographical locations. Through various digital platforms, organizations can encourage collaboration and create a sense of community among employees, even if they are working remotely or in different departments. By embracing technology, organizations can create virtual spaces where employees can exchange ideas, share best practices, and foster a sense of belonging.

Additionally, technology can enhance employee engagement by providing opportunities for personalized learning and development. Online training programs and e-learning platforms allow employees to acquire new skills and knowledge at their own pace, empowering them to take ownership of their professional growth. By investing in technology-driven learning initiatives, organizations can demonstrate their commitment to employee development and create a culture of continuous learning.

Furthermore, technology can streamline processes and boost productivity, freeing up employees' time to focus on tasks that truly add value. Automation and digital tools can help eliminate repetitive and mundane tasks, enabling employees to dedicate their energy to more meaningful and creative endeavors. This not only increases job satisfaction but also enhances employee engagement by aligning their roles with their passions and strengths.

However, it is important to strike a balance between embracing technology and maintaining human connection. While technology can enhance engagement, it should not replace face-to-face interactions entirely. It is crucial for organizations to create opportunities for employees to come together physically, fostering a sense of camaraderie and teamwork.

In conclusion, technology has the power to revolutionize employee engagement and strengthen teams. By embracing technology, organizations can break down barriers, foster collaboration, and provide personalized learning opportunities. Technology-driven processes can also boost productivity and job satisfaction. However, it is important to remember that technology should be used as a tool to enhance human connection, rather than replace it. By striking this balance, organizations can leverage the power of technology to build stronger teams and boost employee engagement, ultimately driving success in the ever-evolving world of organizational behavior.

# The Role of Artificial Intelligence in Engagement

In today's rapidly evolving technological landscape, artificial intelligence (AI) has emerged as a powerful tool with the potential to revolutionize various aspects of our lives. One such area where AI can play a significant role is in enhancing employee engagement within organizations. In this subchapter, we will explore the transformative impact of AI on engagement and how it can contribute to building stronger teams.

Artificial intelligence, at its core, is about utilizing machines to simulate human intelligence and perform tasks that typically require human intervention. When applied to the realm of engagement, AI has the potential to streamline processes, improve communication, and offer personalized experiences, ultimately leading to higher levels of engagement among employees.

One of the key ways AI can enhance engagement is through its ability to automate mundane and repetitive tasks. By automating these tasks, employees can focus on more meaningful and challenging work, which can lead to increased job satisfaction and motivation. Additionally, AI-powered chatbots can provide instant support and answer frequently asked questions, reducing the burden on HR departments and enabling employees to access information quickly and efficiently.

Furthermore, AI can play a pivotal role in communication and collaboration within teams. With the advent of virtual assistants and AI-powered communication platforms, employees can seamlessly connect with their peers, share ideas, and collaborate on projects regardless of their physical location. This fosters a sense of inclusivity and teamwork, promoting engagement and productivity.

Personalization is another area where AI can significantly contribute to engagement. By leveraging AI algorithms, organizations can analyze vast amounts of data to gain insights into individual preferences, strengths, and weaknesses. This enables them to tailor learning and development opportunities, recognition programs, and career paths to each employee's unique needs, fostering a sense of personal growth and engagement.

While AI undoubtedly offers immense potential, it is crucial to strike a balance between automation and human interaction. Organizations must be mindful of creating an environment where employees feel valued and supported, rather than replaced by technology. AI should be viewed as a tool to augment human capabilities, allowing employees to focus on tasks that require creativity, critical thinking, and emotional intelligence.

In conclusion, artificial intelligence has the power to transform employee engagement within organizations. By automating mundane tasks, facilitating communication and collaboration, and enabling personalization, AI can create a more engaging and fulfilling work environment. However, it is essential to approach AI implementation with caution and ensure that the human element remains at the core of any engagement initiatives. Embracing AI as a supportive tool can lead to stronger teams, increased productivity, and ultimately, a more engaged workforce.

# Cultivating a Culture of Lifelong Engagement

In today's fast-paced and ever-changing work environment, it is crucial for organizations to foster a culture of lifelong engagement. This subchapter explores the importance of creating an environment that encourages continuous learning, growth, and development for all individuals within an organization.

Lifelong engagement is not limited to any specific age group or level of experience. It is a mindset that should be embraced by everyone, from entry-level employees to senior executives. By cultivating a culture of lifelong engagement, organizations can enhance employee satisfaction, boost productivity, and foster innovation.

One of the key aspects of creating such a culture is providing ample opportunities for learning and development. This includes offering training programs, workshops, and seminars that cater to different skill sets and interests. By investing in the growth of their employees, organizations demonstrate a commitment to their professional development and overall success.

Additionally, fostering a culture of lifelong engagement requires creating an environment that encourages open communication and collaboration. Employees should feel comfortable sharing their ideas and opinions, knowing that their voices will be heard and valued. This not only enhances employee engagement but also promotes a sense of ownership and accountability within the organization.

Another vital component of cultivating lifelong engagement is the recognition and celebration of achievements. When individuals' efforts are acknowledged and rewarded, they are more likely to be motivated to continue their pursuit of excellence. This can be done through regular performance evaluations, incentive programs, or even simple gestures such as public recognition.

Moreover, organizations should embrace a growth mindset, emphasizing the importance of learning from both successes and failures. Encouraging individuals to take risks, learn from their mistakes, and continuously improve is essential for cultivating a culture of lifelong engagement.

In conclusion, cultivating a culture of lifelong engagement is vital for organizations to thrive in today's dynamic business landscape. By providing opportunities for continuous learning, fostering open communication and collaboration, recognizing achievements, and embracing a growth mindset, organizations can create an environment that promotes employee engagement and drives long-term success. Regardless of age or level of experience, every individual within an organization can contribute to and benefit from a culture of lifelong engagement.

# Chapter 10: Conclusion: Taking Action for Lasting Engagement

## Reflecting on the Power of Connection

In today's fast-paced and digitally-driven world, it is easy to overlook the importance of human connection. However, when it comes to organizational behavior, the power of connection cannot be underestimated. In this subchapter, we will delve into the significance of connection within teams and how it can boost employee engagement and foster a stronger work environment.

Connection goes beyond mere communication; it is about understanding, empathy, and building meaningful relationships. When individuals within a team connect on a deeper level, they are more likely to collaborate effectively, share ideas, and support one another. This ultimately leads to higher productivity and improved outcomes. Research has consistently shown that teams with strong connections perform better, are more innovative, and have higher levels of job satisfaction.

One of the key factors that contribute to the power of connection is trust. When team members trust each other, they feel safe to express their ideas and opinions, take risks, and provide constructive feedback. Trust is built through open and honest communication, active listening, and respecting each other's perspectives. By fostering a culture of trust, organizations can create an environment where individuals feel valued and empowered, leading to increased engagement and motivation.

Connection also plays a vital role in employee engagement. When employees feel connected to their colleagues and the organization as a whole, they are more likely to be committed, loyal, and enthusiastic about their work. This sense of belonging boosts morale and reduces turnover rates, as individuals feel a sense of purpose and fulfillment in their roles.

To harness the power of connection, organizations must prioritize creating opportunities for employees to connect. This can be achieved through team-building activities, mentorship programs, and fostering a collaborative work culture. Additionally, leaders must lead by example, demonstrating the importance of connection through their own actions and behaviors. Encouraging open communication, recognizing and appreciating individual contributions, and providing support and guidance are all essential in building strong connections within teams.

In conclusion, reflecting on the power of connection is crucial for organizations seeking to improve their organizational behavior and boost employee engagement. By fostering trust, promoting open communication, and creating a culture of connection, organizations can tap into the potential of their teams, leading to increased productivity, innovation, and overall success. The benefits of connection extend beyond the workplace, as individuals who feel connected to their colleagues and organization experience greater job satisfaction and personal fulfillment. Embracing the power of connection is not only a smart business strategy but also a fundamental aspect of building a thriving and harmonious work environment.

# Creating a Personalized Engagement Plan

In today's fast-paced and ever-changing work environment, employee engagement has become a critical factor in the success of organizations. A highly engaged workforce not only leads to increased productivity and profitability but also fosters a positive and inclusive work culture. To achieve this, organizations must recognize the importance of creating personalized engagement plans that cater to the unique needs and preferences of their employees.

Understanding that every individual is motivated by different factors is the first step in creating a personalized engagement plan. By conducting surveys, interviews, and focus groups, organizations can gather invaluable insights into what drives their employees and what they value most in their work. This information can then be used to tailor engagement strategies that resonate with each individual.

One effective way to personalize engagement is by allowing employees to have a say in their work arrangements. Flexibility in terms of working hours, remote work options, or job sharing can significantly enhance job satisfaction and work-life balance. By accommodating individual preferences, organizations can demonstrate that they value their employees' well-being and are committed to supporting their individual needs.

Another crucial aspect of a personalized engagement plan is career development. Employees are more likely to be engaged when they see a clear growth trajectory within the organization. Offering opportunities for learning and development, mentorship programs, and regular feedback sessions can help employees feel valued and invested in their professional growth. By aligning employees' career aspirations with organizational goals, organizations can create a win-win situation, where both the individual and the organization benefit.

Recognition and rewards are also essential components of a personalized engagement plan. While some employees may prefer public recognition, others may appreciate a more private acknowledgment. By understanding the different ways in which individuals feel appreciated, organizations can create a culture of recognition that motivates and engages employees.

Lastly, communication plays a vital role in personalized engagement. Regular and transparent communication channels ensure that employees feel informed, included, and connected to the organization. Employers should encourage open dialogue, provide opportunities for feedback, and be responsive to employee concerns.

In conclusion, creating a personalized engagement plan is vital to building stronger teams and boosting employee engagement. By understanding individual motivations, offering flexible work arrangements, providing growth opportunities, recognizing achievements, and fostering open communication, organizations can create an environment where every employee feels valued and motivated to contribute their best. When employees are engaged, organizations thrive, and individuals experience a sense of fulfillment and satisfaction in their work.

## Committing to Continuous Improvement

In today's fast-paced and ever-changing world, organizations must adapt and evolve to stay competitive. This requires a commitment to continuous improvement, a process of constantly assessing and enhancing organizational practices to achieve higher levels of efficiency, productivity, and employee engagement. In this subchapter, we will explore the importance of committing to continuous improvement and how it can benefit both individuals and organizations.

Continuous improvement is not just a buzzword; it is a mindset that should be ingrained in every individual within an organization. It starts with recognizing that there is always room for improvement, regardless of how efficient or successful a process may seem. By embracing this mindset, individuals become open to learning, feedback, and new ideas. They are willing to challenge the status quo and seek innovative solutions to problems. This not only helps organizations stay ahead of the curve but also allows individuals to grow and develop their skills.

One of the key benefits of committing to continuous improvement is increased employee engagement. When individuals feel that their opinions are valued and that they have a voice in shaping the organization's future, they become more invested in the company's success. This leads to higher levels of motivation, job satisfaction, and productivity. By creating a culture that encourages and rewards continuous improvement, organizations can foster a sense of ownership and commitment among their employees.

Continuous improvement also leads to better organizational performance. By regularly reviewing and refining processes, organizations can identify inefficiencies and bottlenecks and implement changes that drive productivity and effectiveness. This can result in cost savings, increased customer satisfaction, and a competitive advantage in the market. Furthermore, the process of continuous improvement encourages organizations to stay agile and adaptable, enabling them to respond quickly to changes in the business environment.

To effectively commit to continuous improvement, organizations must establish a framework that supports this mindset. This includes providing employees with the necessary training and resources to develop their skills, creating a culture that encourages experimentation and risk-taking, and establishing mechanisms for gathering and implementing feedback. By investing in continuous improvement, organizations can create a positive and dynamic work environment where individuals thrive and contribute their best.

In conclusion, committing to continuous improvement is essential for organizations seeking to stay relevant and competitive in today's dynamic business landscape. By embracing this mindset, individuals can grow and develop their skills, leading to increased employee engagement and overall organizational success. By fostering a culture that encourages and rewards continuous improvement, organizations can create a workplace that empowers individuals and drives innovation.

# Inspiring Others to Build Stronger Teams

Building a strong and cohesive team is essential for any organization's success, as it fosters collaboration, creativity, and productivity. However, it is not always easy to get everyone on board and working together towards a common goal. That's where the power of inspiration comes in.

In this subchapter, we will explore effective strategies to inspire others and encourage them to build stronger teams. These strategies are applicable to all individuals, regardless of their position within an organization, making them valuable for anyone interested in organizational behavior.

One of the first steps to inspiring others is leading by example. As a leader, it is crucial to demonstrate the qualities and behaviors you wish to see in your team members. By displaying enthusiasm, dedication, and a strong work ethic, you will inspire others to do the same.

Another powerful way to inspire others is through effective communication. Clearly and passionately expressing your vision and goals for the team will motivate others to contribute their best efforts. Additionally, active listening and providing constructive feedback will foster trust and collaboration within the team.

Recognizing and celebrating the achievements of individuals and the team as a whole is another effective strategy. Everyone wants to feel valued and appreciated, and acknowledging their hard work boosts morale and motivates team members to continue giving their best.

Moreover, encouraging personal and professional growth is essential to inspire others. Providing opportunities for skill development, training, and mentoring not only enhances individual capabilities but also strengthens the team as a whole. When team members feel supported in their growth, they become more engaged and committed to the team's success.

Lastly, fostering a positive and inclusive team culture is crucial for building stronger teams. Encouraging open communication, embracing diversity, and creating a safe space for ideas and opinions will inspire team members to actively contribute their unique perspectives, leading to more innovative solutions and better outcomes.

In conclusion, inspiring others to build stronger teams is a vital aspect of organizational behavior. By leading by example, communicating effectively, recognizing achievements, encouraging growth, and fostering a positive team culture, individuals can inspire and motivate their team members to work together towards shared goals. These strategies are applicable to everyone, regardless of their position, and have the potential to transform teams and boost employee engagement.

# Empowering Employees for a Brighter Future

In today's rapidly changing business landscape, organizations must recognize the importance of empowering their employees for long-term success. In this subchapter, we will explore the significance of employee empowerment and how it can contribute to building stronger teams and boosting overall employee engagement.

Employee empowerment refers to the process of granting employees the autonomy, authority, and resources to make decisions and take ownership of their work. It goes beyond simply delegating tasks; it involves creating a culture that fosters trust, collaboration, and innovation. When employees feel empowered, they become more motivated, productive, and committed to the organization's goals.

One of the key benefits of employee empowerment is the creation of stronger teams. By empowering individuals to make decisions and contribute their unique perspectives, organizations can tap into a wealth of diverse ideas and insights. This leads to better problem-solving, increased creativity, and a more dynamic workplace environment. When employees feel valued and empowered, they are more likely to collaborate, share knowledge, and support one another, resulting in stronger, more cohesive teams.

Furthermore, employee empowerment is closely linked to higher levels of employee engagement. When individuals are given the freedom to make decisions and take ownership of their work, they feel a greater sense of purpose and fulfillment. This, in turn, leads to increased job satisfaction, higher levels of commitment, and reduced turnover rates. Empowered employees are also more likely to be proactive and take initiative, driving innovation and continuous improvement within the organization.

To empower employees effectively, organizations must provide the necessary support and resources. This includes regular communication, training and development opportunities, and access to information and technology. Additionally, leaders must create a supportive and inclusive environment that encourages open dialogue, recognizes and rewards achievements, and values employee input.

In conclusion, empowering employees is essential for building stronger teams and boosting employee engagement. By granting individuals the autonomy and authority to make decisions, organizations can tap into their full potential and drive performance to new heights. Empowered employees are more motivated, productive, and committed, leading to greater innovation, enhanced teamwork, and ultimately, a brighter future for the organization as a whole.

Printed in the USA
CPSIA information can be obtained
at www.ICGtesting.com
CBHW061403070824
12786CB00021B/1190

9 798869 042170